LET
MY PEOPLE
LIVE!

LET
MY PEOPLE
LIVE!

An Indictment

by

Dagobert D. Runes

Philosophical Library
NEW YORK

Manufactured in the United States of America

Instead of a Preface

The one and only Pope ever to speak out in behalf of the Jews, Pope John XXIII before his death had composed a *Prayer of Repentance* in which this true vicar of Christ begged God's forgiveness for the untold suffering brought upon the Jewish nation by the members of the Catholic Church. On his deathbed the Pontiff urged that this prayer be said in all Catholic places of worship. Up to now, this has not been done; the good Pope's wish should be neglected no longer.

Quoting from Pope John's *Prayer of Repentance:*

> *"We admit that over hundreds of years our eyes were blinded, so as not to see the Beauty of Thy Chosen People and not to recognize the features of our firstborn brother. We admit that the sign of Cain is upon our forehead. For centuries Abel was lying in blood and tears while we had forgotten Thy love. Forgive us, O Lord, the curse we unjustly spoke out over the people of Israel. Forgive us, that in their flesh we crucified You the second time! We did not know what we were doing. . . ."*

A Word to the Reader

This composition before you is not a book. Rather is it a historical and philosophical brief demonstrating the fact that the Christian Bible, commonly referred to as the New Testament, contains 102 references to the Jews or the Hebrew people of most degrading, malevolent and libelous kind, thereby creating in the minds and hearts of the Christian children and Christian adults ineradicable hatred towards the Jewish people.

This hatred has brought about during the last two thousand years the killing of almost ten million members of the Jewish race and nation. My wish, with this composition before you, is to prevail upon the Christian people, especially the theologians, teachers and clergymen among them, to work for the elimination of these ugly anti-Semitic references from the Christian Bible. Whatever merit there is to the Christian Gospels, the vitriolic anti-Semitic statements in their text tend to destroy it.

Teaching to disdain and hate the Jew does not add depth or dignity to the Christian faith and has added indescribable horror to the very existence of the people from whom Jeshu ben Joseph claims ancestry. The mouths of the Jewish children, women and men who were burned alive, cut alive, choked to death, and then denied even the most primitive grace of burial, cry out for Justice. If you teach your children and grandchildren to hate, detest and despise the Jew, they will repeat what you and your ancestors have done for two thousand years: Burn the Jew!

LET
MY PEOPLE
LIVE!

Adversary

Whenever Jesus speaks in the New Testament, unless he is made to speak words placed in his mouth by later Christian scribes seeking to justify their pagan-derived theology, he speaks to specific persons who have come to him with specific questions, or personal problems. Upon occasion, impatient or in the heat of debate, Jesus may refer to a group of people by name—"lawyers," "rich men," "Pharisees," or "publicans" (tax-collectors who served the Roman occupation of Israel). Such are the words—such of them as we may have—of Jeshu ben Joseph, the Hebrew preacher.

Yet, again and again, more than one hundred times, and especially in the Gospel of John, alleged to be an especially beloved follower of Jesus, the cunning scribes who much later contrived the gospel narration, identify those to whom Jesus speaks, those with whom he contends, as "the Jews"—never even "some Jews" or maybe "a few Jews," but always "*the* Jews."

Thus, the Jesus of the New Testament is never opposed by flesh-and-blood folk, but by the collective Adversary, good for all time. It is not without significance to Jews that "the Adversary" became a favorite Christian euphemism for the Devil.

1

Anthropologists

Some decades ago the world appeared astonished that serious Christian scholars in Germany and elsewhere proposed that the Jewish race be exterminated because they were destroying the political and social balance of the globe.

The German scholars won out and the Jews of Europe were obliterated.

But this did not represent a triumph of the new "science" of racial purity, nor its quack university doctors of Aryan superiority; rather was it yet another victory for the poisoning churchly doctors who compiled the New Testament. After millennia of bestsellerdom and constant promotion by the Church, their poisoned sacred book had preconditioned Christian Europe to accept—and ardently wish for—removal of the hated kin and "killers" of Jesus.

Auto Da Fe (1492)

The year Columbus discovered America was also the year Ferdinand and Isabella expelled from Spain all Jews who would not convert, to the number of 200,000. Later, nine thousand *Conversos* or *Marranos* were slaughtered to the accompaniment of Holy Mass.

In the city of Madrid, day after day, a total of nine thousand Jewish men, women and children were tied hand and foot to metal stands and burned alive for allegedly desecrating the Catholic faith. These victims of the fury of the Borgianized Vatican and the fanatical court camarilla of Ferdinand and Isabella were driven to madness and despair by torture with knife and torch, until the final burning of their crumpled bodies appeared as salvation to them.

Nine thousand of the most accomplished Jews of medieval Spain—doctors, savants, knights, merchants and their families—were put to death to satisfy the greed of the rulers and the hate of the Catholic Church.

Hundreds of Europeans, the rich, nobles, and courtiers with their ladies, traveled from as far as Scandinavia to Madrid, not to help the condemned Jews and their wives and children, but to watch the burning of the killers of Christ.

Special loges were erected so the Christian ladies and children would not miss any part of the flaming circus of Israel.

Ad majorem Christi gloriam!

Baal

Gods are an unreliable aegis. Hundreds of thousands of innocent men and women have had their throats cut on the altar of one god or another.

The Aztecs did it, the Incas did it, the Greeks and Carthaginians did it, the Phoenicians and the Romans did it. And the gods helped no one but the priest who wielded the knife. I am glad that they are off their pedestals, those ancient monsters of stone and metal.

But we have monsters of flesh and blood.

Bible

New religions in the Western World have solved the problem of respectability and acceptance by leaning most heavily on the ancient faith of Israel. Israel's religious respectability, the sheer weight of the Old Testament tradition, the heroic and devotional depth and beauty of the books of Moses, the wisdom of King Solomon, the divine profundity of the Psalms, give the new faiths substance, justification.

The Society of Friends, the Mormons, Jehovah's Witnesses, Christian Science, Adventists—the first and foremost, the latest and least of the Jesus cults all have bedded themselves in the eternal nest of the Old Testament. Eight hundred pages of the thousand-page "Christian Bible" are nothing but a reprint of the Old Testament of Moses. And every basic issue of Christianity was bound by the early Christians to the teachings and wisdom of the Old Testament.

The sermons and prayers of Jesus are little more than quotations from the wisdom scrolls of Israel. They differ only when Jesus speaks of himself as the son of God, the magic healer and magic performer. All this Jesus cult was purely Hellenic and alien to the Old Testament, that knew no saints and certainly no mixing of God with the flesh of woman. God is One, God is Eternal, God has no name and no face and none may be given Him by man.

In describing the life of Jesus, the early Christian scribes selected only Jewish names for the followers of Jesus. Jews accepting Jesus as God's son would legitimize belief in him. But there is no acceptable document in scroll or tablet or stone available in the language of the Hebrews to confirm acceptance. Not a single writer or biographer or scholar in a single Hebrew document, while there are thousands in Greek and other languages.

The Jews rejected vigorously the presumption of an Olympic dynasty, of God fathering a child with a woman and making such offspring His official vicar, and so on. And, added to this blasphemy in the eyes of the Jews, was a third form of divinity, the Holy Ghost, with forehead, nose and chin.

The apostles, evangelists and correspondents may have adopted *pro tem* Hebrew names to suggest a very desirable Hebrew background, but whatever they were, their product was Greek, not Hebraic. The Roman

Emperor Constantine, a pagan almost all his life, found it practical to promote the new religion built around the new son of God. Under his successors, the standard Latin edition of the Bible, the Vulgate, became the only acceptable religion of the Roman Reich. But in that successful get-religious-quick scheme the Jews were given only an historical role as the ancient, "chosen people of God."

The Chosen People of God were used to back up the new faith. This heritage was precious to the leaders of early Christianity. It gave them respectability, weight and theological historicity. The Jews had no part in it. They rejected it vehemently, unanimously, and the early Christians turned against the obstreperous Jews and invoked a wave of anti-Semitism that has never ceased until this very day. Ten million Jews have paid with their lives for the religious integrity of Israel.

In the fourth century, as now, the so-called Christian Bible comprised 800 pages of the Old Testament and 200 pages of legends of the immaculate conception, the life and death of Jesus, interspersed with 102 vicious Jew-hating references that are equalled only by Hitler's *Mein Kampf.* The Christian Bible has never ceased to malign and insult the people of Israel as traitors, god-killers, Christ torturers, money changers, temple defamers, bone-breakers, etc., etc.

The Christian Bible is the first and forever hateful maligner of the Jewish people. Indeed, it is the only fundamental religious text that is dedicated to the destruction of a single people. No other text—be it Koran, Vedas, or the Analects of Confucius—not one theological text bears hate toward a single people in its pages. The Christian Bible seems to have one underlying message: humiliate, persecute, eliminate the Jews, since they are the killers of Jesus, the God of the Christians!

Such is the Christian blessing given to children at their baptism. Christian children are nurtured on Jew-hate from the age of six on.

Will they ever remove this hate from their text?

Ever?

Caesar

According to the New Testament, a text prepared in Greek for the eyes of Roman officialdom, one should "render unto Caesar the things which be Caesar's."

But what was Caesar's in Israel? Nothing but the rage of an exploited and suppressed people.

Just as the Judeans wanted no part of a Hellenistic-Olympian Trinity, for Caesar they had only the edge of the sword, and at Massada they died rather than submit.

With the last Judean revolt at Massada began the disintegration of the Roman empire; however, in the other colonies of the Empire, Christianity emerged as sole *religio licita*.

Carpenter from Sleepy Hollow

For those Christians who bear a profound resentment against the Jews because they failed to see the Messiah or Christ in the slender carpenter, if they are sincere, let them test themselves: how they would react to a quiet well-spoken young Torah student who claimed in no uncertain terms to be the one and only gate to God, his father?

8

Well, the general Jewish reaction to the wandering preacher was "No"!

Not a single community or synagogue in ancient Israel accepted Christ or Christianity. The God of the Hebrew nation was One, and the only One, and had no face or voice or statue. He was Eternity!

Everything else to the Jews was Hellenism (or Romanism, if you will) and the whole Olympic mountain to them was an abomination. A small nation that refused to place Caesar's statue in the Temple sanctuary would brook no compromise. And they would die for their faith, as they did at Massada. Indeed, it was the Jews who were crucified by the Romans just as Jesus was.

Jesus may have suffered death as one man; the Jews later died by the millions for no other reason than their being the kin of Jesus. What cruelty of the Christians to destroy all Jewish life because the Hebrews refused to accept a man as God.

Would *you* accept Jesus as God today, were he to wander into your home or workshop or inn? Would you?

Children

And Jesus said: Let the children come to me.

And seventy million German Christians, Protestants and Catholics alike, prodded one million Jewish children into windowless chambers where they were choked to death by poisonous gases.

Thus the gentle Jew of Nazareth was given the flower of his kin, because the New Testament in which he is the sterling and divine figure, demands that all Jews, young as well as old, forever be persecuted as punishment for their ancestors' killing of God.

And the Christians of the world closed their eyes and ears, including the anointed bishops, priests and ministers—Pope Pius XII, himself the Vicar of Christ!—and saw nothing, heard nothing. And when a few shiploads of children arrived by night at ports in Palestine and elsewhere, they were sent back, because they had no proper papers!

Available archives of photo and film material (most of which was taken by Germans and Austrians themselves) show grinning German SS officers distributing candy to Jewish kindergarten children, urging them onward into the deadly gas chambers. After two thousand years, they got even with the Christ-killers by shoving Christ's kin into the stove.

As Hitler wrote to Pope Pius XII, *"Wir setzen fort das Werk der Katholischen Kirche"* (We continue the work of the Catholic Church).

．．．．

Albert Einstein, perhaps the greatest of men of this century, rarely told tales; but the universality of children brought this story to his lips during one of my visits to his home in Princeton. I had taken my twelve-year-old daughter along. We talked first of Spinoza and then about reports trickling in from Europe of Germany's final solution for the "Jewish problem" that had troubled the Church for so many centuries.

His story had been told him by a Swiss woman, who had it directly from a German SS officer. The officer had directed operations in an Austrian extermination camp, but escaped to Switzerland after the following incident:

One of the little Jewish girls entrusted to him to guide to the gas chamber stopped at the entrance steps and asked him, a burly man with a false smile, "What are those stoves over there? Are they baking bread?"

"No, Sarah," he said, still smiling, "they will bake you! In twenty minutes you will be but a smoke curl rising from the chimney."

The girl, Einstein related, looked the SS man straight in his white teeth and whispered: "Why do you burn us? We have done nothing."

"Oh yes," answered the officer, "you killed our Lord Jesus, the son of God."

Again the pale child whispered: "I am a daughter of God. Some day He will order your grandchild to be burned, as you are doing to us!"

The SS man stopped suddenly. He ran back, out of the camp into the open forest, and found his way across the border.

The lady from Switzerland who lent him her home as a refuge related the story exactly as it was told to her.

The sage Einstein smiled sadly: "My friend, your young daughter reminded me so very much of the doomed little girl described by the lady from Switzerland.

"Why do they use the name of Jesus to martyr his innocent kin?"

Chosen People

To be a Jew is not only a matter of religion, it is a matter of vocation. The Jew is a chosen guard of the faith of Israel and the people of Israel. Those who fail in their duty are deserters from their nation.

11

Christ the Jew

Christianity is a colorful rainbow of faith centering about the lonely figure of Jeshu ben Joseph, a young carpenter, son of a carpenter living in Israel. Small groups of fishermen, shepherds, farmers and tradesmen took the wandering Talmudically gifted youth for the long-expected *Messiah* who would bring freedom to Israel and Toraic righteousness to the sons of Jacob.

Christianity in its initial decades was nothing but this Messianism of devout Judaism. The word "Christ" is but the Greek equivalent *(Christos)* for the Hebrew *Messiah.*

Jeshu ben Joseph never uttered the word "Christ" in his sermons or talks, nor did he ever refer to himself as Jesus, the Greek "translation" of Jeshu.

Indeed, neither did Shimon ever speak the name "Peter" as his own, or Jochanan the name "John," or Saul the name "Paul."

These names were Greek to them, even as they were to Jeshu. Jews in Israel spoke Aramaic or Hebrew; only around Caesarea in the north was Greek spoken and written by immigrants from Greece, and Latin only by the occupying Roman police forces of south Syria, of which Israel was part.

Were I to show to Jeshu my Greek copy of the New Testament he would undoubtedly look at it bewildered. He would hardly recognize any of the names in the to him utterly strange "Christian Bible," written in an alien tongue filled with saintly cognomens for persons whom he knew as gentle, trusty Hebrew farmers and fishermen.

In the fourth century of our era, the Emperor Constantine the Great decided for political reasons (the king remained a "pagan" until his dying days) to raise "Messianity" to the dignity of *religio licita* in the Roman Empire. He ordered the Bishops to present in good form the life and lore of the Messiah (Christos) in a Book (Biblion), which has ever since been accepted in the rapidly expanding Christian Empire as the "New Testament."

The Old one, that into which Jeshu was born, the one which governed his life and preachings as a Jew among Jews, the one whose laws he observed from becoming Bar Mitzvah to the much-illustrated Holy Meal, the one whose bitter lament he cited *(Eli, Eli, Lami Sabbatanu)*—this, the Old Testament, the Greek and Roman masters of the later Catholic Church relegated to the embarrassing ruins of their heritage.

However, the New Testament is a book written entirely by Jewish persons, whom no Greek or Roman references can change to "gentiles," whatever that word implies.

It is interesting to note that all writings of the Christian Bible were originally composed by Jewish believers in the Jewish Messiah. Indeed, Saul whom the Roman masters of their new Church called "Saint Paul," in his earlier years considered circumcision as an essential part of the conversion of a pagan to Christianity. It is one of the great tragicomedies of history that the Jews who made the New Testament were its bloody victims and that in 102 places of this Roman-edited Messianic volume, in 102 places the Jew is mocked, accused, insulted, accursed, libelled—indeed, set up for open massacre by the alleged curse of Jesus: You are the sons of the Devil and do the Devil's lust.

God's chosen people have been ripped from the protection of the Lord and turned over to the scum of

13

"Christianity" to have its nefarious will with them. And among the ten million Jews the Christians have put to death are the very descendants of Jesus, his father and mother, his brothers and sister, his blood cousins and neighbors.

The Jew-hate of the Christian Church is based upon a New Testament prepared three hundred years after the event by scribes of the Roman Bishops in the Greek language, which was totally unknown to the Hebrew shepherds and fishermen who served as Jesus' apostles and evangelists. This hate has been and still is shared by the ugly references to the "Jews" the god killers, the god torturers, the god betrayers, in the pages of the "New" Testament. The New Testament in its hate of everything Jewish is not even surpassed by Hitler's *Mein Kampf.*

Every reference to the Jews in the "New Testament" is contemptuous, hateful, derisive. This alleged book of love preaches nothing but hate to God's own people—these are God's words, not mine. God called the Jews His Chosen People, although of late Pope Pius XII and the Vatican endeavored to take the title "chosen people" for those persons who confess to the Catholic Church.

It is unbelievable that in this twentieth century hundreds of millions of Christians continue to teach devilish hate of all Jews, dead and still unborn, to their fellow religionists.

Yet Jesus called himself Messiah (Christ) of the Jewish nation. No other nation had or has a Messiah or expected one. To reiterate, Messiah is a Jewish idea, Jewish hope and Jewish belief. Jesus came, he believed, to help his people in time of their suppression.

Jesus was not a Roman or Italian or Greek; he was a

Jew deeply involved in the Jewish faith, wore the Hebrew religious clothing, cut his hair like a Jew, kept the Jewish holidays and rituals as a Jew. He spoke for his people who lived under Roman oppression, and the Romans killed him even as, a hundred years later, they wiped out thousands of Jesus' countrymen at Massada.

The Roman bishops put together an alleged life of Jesus in Greek, Rome's intellectual lingo, and to take the onus away from the Roman imperialists, the bishops in the service of Emperor Constantine, a pagan, inserted a version that would blame the Jews for the Roman execution of Jesus. The Romans habitually crucified political prisoners and the killing of Jesus was not an exception or rare case.

But to seize, as the Christians of Europe did in our time, and poison a million Jewish children for Christ's sake, is an abomination the like of which the world has never seen.

And how the Christian fascists, no matter what their denomination, swarmed all over Europe—France, Italy, the Ukraine, Poland, Austria, Germany, Hungary, Holland—to round up Jewish women, children and defenseless men, to drag them to Germany for execution!

Churchgoers

Church attendance in Hitler Germany and Austria was, on the average, eight percent higher than in previous years. The Jewish people living in those two Germanic countries represented only a minor fraction of the population, and a notably loyal, talented, and productive fraction. Yet, so effective were the anti-Semitic interpolations in the New Testament that the

15

cannibalism of the German state against its Jewish citizens appeared as no more than a punitive cleansing process visited upon the God-killers.

Coexistence

between Christians and Jews is made difficult from childhood by the teachings of the Christian Sunday schools as well as gospel-based instructions.

The New Testament pictures the Jew as a venomous killer of God, thus creating and perpetuating in Christian children the image of the Ugly Jew.

This image never really leaves the Christian. Most Christians live their lives with these malevolent falsehoods and die with them:

—The Jews are the Sons of the Devil and do the Devil's lust.

—Jesus asked the Jews: Why do you seek to kill me?

—The Jews pleaded with Pilatus to break the legs of the dying Jesus to hasten his death.

—Jesus said: You brood of Abraham are desirous of murdering me.

As long as this "Bible" is not cleansed of its ferocious anti-Semitism, the Jews cannot peacefully coexist with their Christian neighbors.

Constantine

was many years of his life embattled with sundry Roman *Augusti* and Co-Caesars for the supreme military power over Italy and the other Roman lands. He finally won, perhaps with help from the early Christian segments of the population.

His victory was sealed in 312 when he smashed his

competitor Maxentius at the Milvian Bridge over the Tiber River. Cross-bearing Christians seem to have assisted him in this particular encounter, probably because he had shown sympathy for the Jesus-followers. Maxentius, his last powerful opponent, was drowned in the rout. Suddenly the Jesus followers found themselves a favored group. Largely because of Constantine's toleration and sympathy, Christianity became the new focus of religious attraction and propaganda.

Constantine took it upon himself to regulate the doubtful issues of the early Church, to unify its principles in councils and meetings, and establish the Catholic Church with a hierarchy of bishops.

In Greece and other Mediterranean lands, the new faith swept the pagan gods off the places of worship and substituted Christian service and obedience by the beginning of the fifth century. Pagan deities of stone were decapitated, amputated and buried or thrown in the nearest bay.

Christianity won by edict of the emperors, from Iberia to Syria, from Ethiopia to Scotland.

The only nation that rejected the Jesus cult were the Hebrews who opposed vehemently the Hellenistic theology of God's fatherhood and Mother Mary's mysterious motherhood. The Jews said "No" to the Jesus cult and ridiculed the new idolaters.

It is most significant that the emperor who promoted Christianity as the only tolerable belief was born and remained until on his deathbed a Hellenistic pagan. His successors, nominal Christians, made Christianity the official, then the *only* legal religion in the Roman Reich.

What stands out in these historical events? The founder of the first international Christian Church was a pagan, Constantine. The Caesars who followed Constantine enforced this new faith upon the Roman empire to unify Christian as well as pagan Hellenistic sects under the Roman Imperium.

Hellenistic legends and beliefs were already widely spread around the Mediterranean Sea. What the Imperial theologians did was to combine the ancient spiritual weight of the Old Testament with the Hellenistic legends of God siring a son with a mortal woman, incorporating Logos, Holy Ghost, Gnosis and other Greek mystical concepts with tales of miracle and magic by Jeshu, the son of God. The masses of the already Hellenized empire made no objection to the New Christian Bible, Old and New testaments in one book, all the dejected and cowed peoples of the Roman empire—except the Hebrews.

The Hebrews initiated an intensive emotional and intellectual attack against Christian Hellenism, and wanted no part of it. To the Hebrews, God was One, the Creator of all. The Hebrews found the tale of God's fleshborn son sheer blasphemy and Mary's pregnancy downright paganism. It is highly significant that in authentic Hebrew exegesis and rabbinic literature we find not a single script or scroll in Hebrew of the Christian theology or Jesus-legend.

Early Christianity was defined in Greek by Hellenists; the Jews would not touch it. God was neither a bull nor a swan nor an angel. God was faceless and nameless and His chosen people were the Hebrews, not the Greeks or Iberians or Romans.

When the followers of Moses rejected Christianity root, stock, and branch, the early church fathers became antagonistic, indeed, vituperative against the Jews and what they stood for.

While the Imperial clerics and theologians held on

18

desperately to the ancient Old Testament and even gave Hebrew names to the new saints of the Jesus cult, they simultaneously tried in the Gospels to free the Romans who had crucified Jesus from all guilt for his demise, and turned savagely upon the obstreperous Jews to mark them the sole offenders.

The Jews were blamed, and the Jews only, for the death of God's son; Pilatus, the Roman police chief in southern Syria (Palestine), became a mild defender of Jesus; the Jewish Priests were made-up as bloodthirsty madmen in the official script. The world divides itself in two peoples, the Gentiles and the Jews—and the Jews alone are the killers of God.

No more was the fish, an innocent picto-acronym, the popular symbol of Christianity, but a gallows, the Crucifix!

The life of Jesus became the drama of a hanging, an execution of God's fleshbegotten son, with the Jews as villain, bearing the sole guilt, never to be extirpated.

Conversion

The major part of the Christian Bible, the so-called Old Testament, reiterates, emphasizes and dogmatizes: There is only One God since Eternity and for Eternities. There is no other God besides Him. All other thinking is idolatrous!

In the minor part of the same Christian Bible, referred to as New Testament, there appears a Son of God, a Mother of God, etc. etc.

One must choose: the Hebrew part of the Bible, or the Hellenistic part! The two cannot coexist.

The Hebrews never accepted the Hellenistic part ex-

19

cept in later Christian eras under the threat of burning torches under their feet or their children's feet. Convert or be burned was the gentle message of Christianity throughout history, from Torquemada to Hitler.

Covenant

The Christians in their covenant (New Testament) relentlessly attack "the Jews," *all* Jews, as God killers, money lenders, torturers of Jesus, defilers of the Temple, money-bought traitors, spies and devils.

Why, then, does the Lord speak only Hebrew and only to the Jews? Does the Lord prefer the devils to the Christians? I wonder.

Crucifix

The Romans killed a single Jew, Jesus Christ, and the world justly was enraged; since then the Christians have killed ten million Jews, among them one million children, from the crusades to the Hitler decade, and few Christians intervened or tried to stop the massacre.

The Christian Church made the Crucifix, a saintly Jew (by their own heraldry, a direct descendant of King David) hanging on a Roman cross, the dominant symbol of their faith.

The crucifix has now for two thousand years served as a constant reminder to their faithful that *the* Jews lynched their own kin and therefore are forever outcasts or as Hitler would put it, *Vogelfrei,* subject to retribution and revenge by any true Christian.

The Christian religion is the only one to embody in its

very tenets the perennial hate of one particular nation. Indeed the basic theology of Christianity is a legalistic drama of hate, unto the last generation of Jesus' own people, his kin; hate of the faithful against the God-killers.

Crusades

The relentless emphasis in the books of the New Testament on the alleged persecution of the person of Jeshu by his Jewish contemporaries, their thirst for the blood of Jesus ("and may his blood come upon us and our children") built up in the centuries that followed an explosive resentment in Christian adherents against all persons of the Hebrew race.

In stone and paint, in sermon and hymn, in prayer and procession, the Jew was relentlessly depicted, attacked and defiled as the Son of the Devil.

In the early Middle Ages, the crusades allegedly planned to save the religious relics of the Jesus-cult from the barbaric Moslems, were diverted in Europe into savage pogroms against the men, women and children of Jewish heritage. The bestialities of the Christian Crusaders against the hapless Jews were only equaled by the massacres of the Hitler-inspired Germans.

And when the Crusaders arrived in the City of Jerusalem, they drove the few thousand Jews left into the large Synagogue and burned them alive.

Such fury did the horror tales of the New Testament create in the minds of the Christian masses that they compelled the Christian rulers of Spain, Portugal, England, France and elsewhere to expel the Hebrews from their lands. Of course, in the process thousands and thousands of the kinsmen of Jeshu perished by axe, drowning and the perennial flame of Christian "vengeance."

On March 16, 1190, in York (England) the Jews were driven into the Tower. Fire was set to their house of refuge and they died either in fighting the storming multitudes of Christians or by the flame!

After a thousand years, another Massada.

Not until 1656 were the Jews permitted by Oliver Cromwell admission to England. And those were weary refugees from other Christian countries, Spain and Portugal.

In Spain the Jews had been expelled by the Crown allied with the Holy See in 1492. And of those who accepted Christianity *(marranos)* nine thousand were burned alive, men, women and children.

So deeply had the New Testament infuriated Christian Europe that their mortal suffering and anguish created in the Jesus-people only a sense of gratification: "At last justice was done and the God-killers were suitably punished for crucifying the Son of God." Thus Saint Vincent Ferrer, Dominican and "miracle" converter of Jews in Spain, expressed his contentment.

Deicide

is a rather incongruous word—if God is God, no man can destroy him.

If man, Roman or otherwise, manages to destroy Him, then the destroyer has superdivine powers and God was just a figment of the tired imagination of a Church father or somesuch. This whole fabric of God killing is a wishful tissue of human fancy. You cannot kill God; and if you say someone did, you are pulling people's legs until they fall into a pit of superstition.

If Jeshu ben Joseph was God, the Romans could not have crucified him and watched him die. And so the whole clever drama of Jesus' life and death turns out to be a sad, bad script. Gods don't die, and then rise to heaven; they reside there. It is their perennial abode. Gods don't move, and Jehovah is still where He was three thousand years ago at the time of Moses and where He was five thousand years ago at the time of Noah.

Let's leave things where they belong: Jewish preachers in Israel and the God of those chosen people of His in heaven above the River Jordan. And if the bishops of Rome who contrived the gospel of the God who dies have a grudge against the Jews, let them think up a more plausible excuse than a dying God on the gallows.

23

The Romans of old never were short of alibis for condemning a nation or for persecuting a people. I for one propose to scrap the script of the murdered God and replace it with something more serious, such as "Israel and what it has done for the world in five thousand years."

Devil Jews

Jesus preached: "Ye are of your father the devil, and the lusts of your father ye will do. He was a murderer from the beginning, and abode not in the truth, because there is no truth in him. He is a liar and the father of lies."

Thus teaches the New Testament wisdom about Israel! Thus, to the Christian child every Jew is a devil and son of a devil.

Ecce Homo

There is no knowledge of the face of Jesus or his body. Yet there abound a thousand million pictures of this legendary carpenter. His trade should have given him powerful arms and shoulders.

What are all those likenesses of a tall, thin, Nordic-looking young man but expressions of an anxiety among Christians to get away from a Hebrew image of Jesus? The ancient Hebrews were as a whole neither blond, nor particularly tall or thin. They were Oriental-looking, like their Arab cousins.

The Roman clergy responsible for putting together the New Testament believed in making the followers of Jesus as non-Jewish as possible. (Only the traitor Iscariot was endowed with the cognomen "Judas"—a broad hint!)

So most Christians do not know that there never walked in ancient Israel a man called "Jesus"; Jeshu ben Joseph, perhaps. And no "Peter" and no "Paul"; perhaps Shimon, a fisherman, and Saul, the Torah student. Indeed, if Jeshu were to return today, he would not turn around were someone to call out "Jesus," nor would Shimon drop his net if someone yelled "Peter!"

These men were not Greeks; they spoke Hebrew only, or Aramaic, wore the typical Jewish garb, cut their hair in prescribed traditional manner, earlocks and all; with their tassled shirts beating about their hips, they murmured the conventional Hebrew blessings before and after eating, refrained from sitting next to a woman, or from drinking milk with their meat.

Were you to show the apostles a scroll of the original Greek New Testament, being simple men, they would be unlikely even to guess the language it was written in. They were simple men and to them there was only one holy language, Hebrew, the tongue in which the Lord spoke to Moses.

And Jesus, despite the wish-fulfilling paintings and drawings, was not a German or a Swede or a Pole. The *dramatis personae* of the New Testament are Jewish men and women; it is time you control your hates and change your images.

When Michelangelo wanted a model for his Piéta, he went to the Jewish ghetto in Rome and selected a Jewish student.

If *you* want to paint or sculpt the figures of the New Testament, go to the Warsaw Ghetto (I forget—its inhabitants were all put to death by the followers of Christ, save a few that escaped, who were expelled by the Poles, also believers in Christ.)

Well, if you want to help your imagination, then go to Tel Aviv; there you will find descendants of King David, like Joseph, the father of Jeshu.

Whatever he was—rabbi, carpenter, or fanatic—Jeshu was of the Hebrew flesh and blood, so don't paint him in the image of the European assassins of his people!

Fathers of the Church

It is, of course, difficult to write of such men as the early Church Fathers with that frank directness one can employ in dealing with historic figures whose pictures one can see without halos around their heads.

While this halo surrounding the early Church Fathers did inspire a great number of followers of the Christian faith to piety or intense religious observance, to the Jews that halo emanated only a flame of hatred, and in a thousand cases, nay, in a thousand times a thousand cases, this is to be taken literally.

The Church Fathers were not sophisticated scholars and historians; they were ready to accept the elaborate tale of crucifixion publicized in the early versions of the Synoptics and soundly Jew-hating John, as well as the mass of letters from the pen of the irrepressible Paulus. Himself a renegade, after his lightning conversion he quickly turned from a witness, or martyr, of Judaism to a relentless apostle of Judeo-Christianity.

After Paulus' turning away from and against his own people, not only theologically but also racially, the burden of building the new Christian edifice quickly was shifted from the shoulders of the early Judeo-Christians to the pagan and Roman Christians, who found it most practical to look upon Jesus, not as another prophetic or heretic figure of Israel, but rather as a god of the Roman world whom the sinister Jews assassinated. Within decades the very people of Jesus, Mary and Joseph became anathema. The true history of the growth and life of early Judeo-Christianity was pushed into darkness and a set of fantastic legends became Gospel Truth in all their animosity against the very people of Jeshu ben Joseph.

The early Church Fathers were patchwork theologians, floundering in this new Christianity that had spread like wildfire among the lowly people of the Roman Empire; broken by scores of dissident sects and mutual accusations of heresy, united not even by the concept of trinity; imbued, however, by one profound emotion—insatiable, violent and pitiless hate against the accursed People of the Book.

Let's see what some of the benimbused saints have to say of the Lord's chosen people:

Justin Martyr, who was executed in Rome in 167 for his Christian beliefs, in his appeal to Marcus Aurelius accused the Jews of inciting the Romans to kill the Christians after they had murdered God. In his "Dialogue with Trypho," he wishes that the country of the Jews be rendered a desert and their towns be consumed by flames, that their enemies may eat the fruit of Israel, and that no Jew ever be able to go to Jerusalem.

Another Christian theologian, martyred by the Romans in 251, was Saint Origen, who contended that the Jews were always envious of the Christians and would never cease to lure their unwary neighbors into their net and destroy those who would oppose their evil designs. In fact, whenever fortune turned away from the Christians this could be traced to the Jews.

Another great and erudite theologian, Eusebius, Bishop of Caesarea, who flourished around 300, maintained steadfastly that the Jews of every community would crucify a Christian at the Purim festival every single year as a public demonstration of their feeling against Jesus. Eusebius further asserted that in the Roman-Persian War the Jews purchased ninety thousand Christian prisoners for the mere pleasure of killing them. This kindly saint at the Council of Nicaea was one of the most powerful architects of Christian dogma. He is also the author of the great ecclesiastical history which is the only source of information for much of that era.

Saint Hilary of Poitiers (died 367) interpreted the Jews historically as a perverse people, forever accursed by God.

Saint Ephraem (died 373), who is held in highest regard by Syrian and other Eastern churches, is the author of a great body of liturgical hymns, a number of which carry maligning references to the Jews, styling their synagogues as whorehouses.

Saint Zeno, fourth-century Bishop and patron saint of Verona, bewailed the fact that when inspired monks invaded Jewish homes to save Holy Scriptures and killed resisting Jews, only the bones of the dead were burned to ashes, while there were still many live Jews about who could have been burned for the glory of the Lord!

Saint Cyril, Patriarch of Alexandria (died 444), a noted dogmatist, gave the Jews a choice of exile or conversion. Those who resisted, including the prefect, were stoned to death.

Saint Jerome (died 420), editor of the Latin *Vulgate* and a dictionary of Christian biographies, "proves" in his "Tractatus Against the Jews" that the Jews are incapable of understanding Holy Scripture and that their lies are driving Christians into heresy. They should therefore be most severely prosecuted until they confess to the true faith. He and Saint Augustine could rightly be called the spiritual fathers of the Medieval Inquisition.

Saint Augustine (died 430), Bishop of Hippo, and by far the most influential man in Christian theology, called Judaism a corruption. "The true image of the Hebrew is Judas Iscariot, who sells the Lord for silver. The Jews can never spiritually understand the Scriptures and forever will bear the guilt for the death of Jesus because their fathers killed the Savior." In the eyes of Saint Augustine, the Jews called upon themselves for all eternity the divine malediction and must be employed in no other capacity than as slaves.

(Martin Luther, who was much inspired by Saint Augustine, went him one better by demanding that the Jews be made slaves of the slaves, because if they were to be merely slaves they would have some contact with German Christians.)

Saint Thomas Aquinas (died 1274), a member of the Dominican Order that had the distinction of being a pillar of the Inquisition, philosophized: "It would be perfectly licit to hold the Jews, because of their crucifying the Lord, in perpetual servitude."

Saint Ambrose, a fourth-century bishop of Milan, one of the four Latin doctors of the church, a standard bearer of Christian ethics, reprimanded Emperor Theodosius, who ordered the rebuilding of a synagogue in Mesopotamia that had been destroyed at the instigation of a rabid monk. In fact he himself offered to burn the synagogue in Milan, if it hadn't been burned already.

Saint Athanasius, a fourth-century bishop of Alexandria, who was honored as the father of orthodoxy, kept insisting that Rome deal with the Jews by use of the sword and that tolerance was no better than treason against Christ.

Saint Cyprian, a third-century bishop of Carthage, the most outstanding churchman of that century, executed by the Romans, demanded that the Jews be driven from the land at the point of the sword.

Many of the princes of Christian Europe for a thousand years and more took the precepts of these learned theologians to heart, treating the Jews of their realm as private chattels, using them often for sordid and exploitative purposes. When discovery threatened, they sacrificed the Jews to the mob.

The mobs of Europe, as well as their semi-literate clergy, grew up in anti-Semitism. They were baptized, not into the loving spirituality of Jesus the Hebrew, but into the venomous and carnal animosity of Jew hatred. Nine out of ten Christians prior to the eighteenth century were totally illiterate. The small minority of thinking people could not reach them, but the priests and ministers had their ear every Sunday of every week, every month of every year.

Every visit to a Christian church became then, as it still often becomes today, a journey to the school of contempt. The Jew was perfidious because he would not accept a visible God. The Jew was nefarious because he held on to the belief that the Lord is One and the Lord is justice and the Lord is charity and the Lord is mercy, and there is no god but the God of Eternity. In fact, if He has a name it is Elohim, *Eternities.* The Jews were accursed—so preached the churches, as they still do—because the "Gospel Truth" reads that some of them, some thousands of years ago, somewhere in Asia, put God to death. What blasphemy all this is!

And for two thousand years, the mobs were ever ready to bleed the Jews, to club the Jews, to burn the Jews. The cardinals urged it, the princes did it—why not the lowly people?

The early Christian Fathers may have been involved cogitators in theology and metaphysics, but to the Jews they carry no halo. They carry searing hatred at the tip of both tongue and pen.

Shall we praise the assassins of our children? Shall we glorify the spiritual fathers of the massacres of our ancestors? Shall we indulge in respectful reverence towards those dark men who twisted the cross into a dagger against our nation?

We have no quarrel with the great message of Jesus, born out of the prophetic wisdom alive in the Israel of his time. But we can have no dialogue with the false and hateful adherents of churches who have for two thousand years used the death of a shining Son of Israel to wound and maim, to cut and burn and choke to death the children of his very brethren.

The Vatican has chosen to beatify, to canonize, and to sanctify the bones of what they call the Fathers of the Church, the illustrious doctors of the faith.

I say, *unum habetis doctorem*—there is only one Rabbi. This is the title that Jesus was addressed by. He spoke neither Roman nor Greek. He was a Hebrew and he had nothing in common with the casuistics of the Greek or Roman speculators in theology. The great message of Jesus is love to all, neighbor and stranger, friend and foe. This is an old teaching of his old people, only he said it so touchingly and so very profoundly.

But the message of the Church Fathers was fire and sword against the whole world of Israel. Jesus lived and perished in a world of Israel, Israel under the boot of the Roman legions, but spiritually free, and Jesus was part of this freedom. His sermons spoke of the world within, of infinite kindness, generosity and charity.

Where is the charity in the writings of the fanatical fathers of this fanatical group of churches? It seems they are certain of nothing in their theology except of the hatefulness of the demon Jew. Henry VIII, the adulterous decapitator, founder and head of the Anglican Church, would have no Jews in England. Neither would Queen Isabella in Spain. And Martin Luther wanted them only in the slave stables. And of the popes I will not speak. Their own historians refused to hide the truth.

There has lately been a lot of talk about a dialogue between Christians and Jews. We don't want to talk to them. We only want them to stop talking against us in their books, in their press, in their speeches, in their sermons, in their homes. We want them to cease playing out the dreadful and hateful drama of the crucifixion of a god who did not die.

Perhaps it doesn't occur to them that there are among our people still the living sons and daughters of the kin of Jesus. How many of them were killed by the church-going Germans of the Hitler era I do not know, but if the kin of Jesus are still living, they attend a synagogue and not a church.

God Himself

And Jesus said to the Jews: "If ye believe not that I am *He,* ye shall die in your sins."

Well, the Jews did not believe that Jesus was God and Christ's words made millions of Jews die.

Graven Images

Why do artists persist in showing Jesus as a baby and his mother as a nursing woman? Is God's baby boy more appealing than God's preaching son?

While we have no idea what Jesus the man looked like, we also lack a likeness of Jesus the infant. What need is met by all these imaginary pictures of God the suckling or God on the Roman gallows?

The Hebrews made no likenesses of God.

Graves

We have found Jewish bodies of the time of Moses, of Abraham and Noah.

But no Jewish bodies of the time of Pope Pius XII—their corpses went into smoke and into soap.

Our sages tell the legend of ancient Israel, that the souls of the murdered righteous who are not given back to God's earth will linger at His side 'til Judgment Day, in order to stand witness against the greatest of evildoers, those who take a man's life and then rob him of eternal rest.

In the last two thousand years the Christians have put an end to the life of ten million Jews. The Germans burned the bodies of six million children, women and men; the Catholic Church those of four million. The Germans burned the Jews after gassing them; the Catholic Church burned the Jews alive, children, women and men.

Even the Huns left fallen enemies to their families for burial. The Christians of modern Europe—Germans, Austrians, French, Ukrainians, Poles—they burned the twisted corpses of the poisoned Jews, as Nazi leader Frank said, "To fart into the countenance of their God Jehovah!"

This did not affect the God of Moses; He had left Europe the day Hitler came to power. Perhaps He left for America, the only Christian country that never killed a Jew for his religion.

Hate

Why don't those Jew-haters, for once, place themselves in the shoes of the hatee? Or, rather than "shoes," in their manacles, their cells, their pyres, their gas chambers?

Hebrew

The only languages Jesus spoke were Hebrew and Aramaic, the very same as his ancestor David the King.

Since we have only early transcripts in Greek of the New Testament, we do not have a single phrase or word that Jesus spoke. The New Testament is a Greek book compiled in Rome hundreds of years after the demise of Jesus. What we have before us are Greek transcripts or translations, assembled in the 4th century by the bishops on the order of the Roman emperor.

The translator into Latin of the dominant Roman Catholic version of the New Testament, commonly known as the *Vulgate,* was Jerome or Hieronymus (346-420) who, far from being a hermit, wandered from Gaul to Egypt invariably with an entourage of inspired ladies. He studied Hebrew to revise the Vulgate's Old Testament section; the New Testament he translated from available Greek manuscripts.

May I reiterate—there is not a single believable record left us of a Hebrew text of the New Testament. Since Jesus spoke Hebrew and Aramaic only, we have no Hebrew heritage of the words of Jesus. We do not have a single authentic sentence from the lips of Jesus.

We have therefore to rely on Greek writers or "translators" for what is presented as *verba Christi*. We have nothing but rewrites by churchbound devotees who set down on paper or tablet a message already three hundred years old and spoken a thousand miles away.

And we all know what writers and translators can do with the words of God, His son or any of God's children.

Hinduism

In its multiple forms has been for decades an escape for millions of European and American Christians in their flight from disillusionment.

Hinduism, Theosophy, Buddhism and Zen can be entered from the shaky grounds of Christianity without actually giving up the Jesus cult. Those doubtful Thomases need not abandon their loose adherence to Christian theology with the godson who walks and preaches, and the Hebrew godfather who is relegated somehow to a grandfather status, and the silent Holy Ghost standing by. Furthermore, there is no mention in the New Testament of Hindus, or Tibetans, or Nipponese. It is perfectly all right to bask in the glow of their theology, dance their dances, repeat their incantations, practice their rituals, or even engage in yoga contortions and sundry other exercises.

In one sentence: All oriental religious rites are perfectly all right—as long as a Christian does not become Judaized, because, as we all know, the Jews tortured Jesus, the firstborn son of God, but the Hindus *et al.* are Gentiles.

Jewish Posse

"Then the band and the captain and the officers of the Jews seized Jesus and bound him." They took him to the Jewish high priest Caiaphas. The Gospel of John continues: "Now Caiaphas was he which gave counsel to the Jews that it was expedient that one man should die for the people."

Thus reads the account of Jesus' arrest fabricated by the bishops of Rome—complete with an insinuation of ritual sacrifice! And this tale has been repeated to Christian children in Sunday schools, century after century, until the young are filled with hate and fury against all children of Israel.

Judea

"Jesus would not walk in Judea, because the Jews sought to kill him"—so wrote John (VII:1).

Then where did Jesus walk? In Galilee, John reports. And who lived in Galilee—Gentiles?

Killer Jews

And Jesus cried out to the Jews: "Why go ye about to kill me?" (John VII:19)

And how does such a despairing cry affect Christian children at Bible lesson? What impression does it create in Christians?

Literature

French, German and Russian literature—all have drunk deep at the Gospel cauldron of evangelic Jew hate.

The Frenchman Drumont proposed the pillaging of Jews with the support of much of the French clergy. Similarly, German philosophy, led by men like Kant, Hegel, Herder, Fichte, Heidegger, absorbed much of the poisonous Jew-hate prevalent in the Christian Bible, and of course, in the speeches and sermons of Martin Luther who wanted the houses and Talmuds of the Jews burned.

Through its impact upon the philosophers, writers, and teachers, the anti-Semitism contained in the Roman Christian Bible has infected all of the Western World.

None of the world's other religions have it, or had it. Anti-Semitism is born with the Christian Church and can only die if the Church cleanses its pages of this bloody element.

Love Thine Enemy

The Christians quote Jesus: Love thine enemy! So why do they still kill the Jews?

Because Christian duty is to love one Jew, Jesus, and

41

hate all the others as incarnation of the Devil (John VIII: 44).

On the positive side, words—a million times prayerfully repeated expressions of charity toward abstract humanity in the name of Jesus, the gentle Jew of Nazareth.

In reality, killing—ten million Jews slain by Gospel-infuriated Christians. Among the victims, one million Jewish children choked to death by "cultured" Germans of both the Catholic and Lutheran faiths, with the assistance of French, Austrian, Polish and Ukrainian "Jesus-followers."

(Of course, in addition to the Hebrews, the Christians massacred by flame and rack hundreds of thousands of witches, heretics and pagans, such as Aztecs, Incas, Asians and Africans. Brothers of "holy" orders as the Dominicans and Franciscans served as a Gestapo, in charge of the torture chambers of the Vatican judicial branch.)

To the Vatican, the Jew was and is personification of the infamy of killing God. The New Testament did—and still does!—hold every Jewish infant of every era responsible for the alleged demise of God's first-born son.

Is it surprising that even after the military debacle of Hitler, Pétain, etc., the Vatican, especially, was opposed to "Jewish revenge"? The Holy See advocated "Christian forgiveness" for the Nazi criminals and until the Eichmann apprehension, gave out Vatican passports to scores of the German Jew-killers as an act of mercy!

What "wondrous love"!

Luther

Luther gave his life to the purification of Christianity; yet he was among the most fanatical anti-Semites, perhaps because he advocated a return to the "purity" of the Gospels!

He thundered to his listeners to "burn the Talmuds of the Jews" and drive them from *Haus und Hof.* He even admonished the Germans not to seek out a Jewish physician—he would poison them!

Marxism

like National Socialism derived its attitude toward the Jews directly from the New Testament.

Indeed, way back in 1936 Hitler advised Pope Pius XII that he felt himself burdened with the same responsibility as the Vicar of Christ, namely, to segregate Jews and Judaism and work toward their elimination.

Karl Marx, while born of Jewish parents, was baptized by them at the age of six into Lutheranism and received a strongly anti-Semitic Protestant education in his school years.

As Marx explained in his book *Probleme zur Judenfrage* (published in America under the title *A World Without Jews)*, "The God of the Jews is money; the profession of the Jew is usury."

So wrote this malicious little convert grandson of a Rabbi.

Mass

The Christian is told that the wine drunk at that holy occasion is actually Christ's blood. In Medieval times, Jews were accused by the Catholic clergy of killing Christian children and drinking their blood!

Writers like Chaucer even poetized this vulgar slander and throughout the English-speaking world this monstrous lie is read by students and teachers, how Jews apprehend a Christian child, cut its throat and suck its blood!

Why is it that the Christians must always create a Jewish enemy to confirm writ and ritual of their sacrificial God-king drama?

Miracles

are no longer palatable to modern man; so he relegates them to a convenient past, but with their hateful implications for a living people unrevised.

Money Changers

"And the Jews' passover was at hand, and Jesus went up to Jerusalem and found in the temple those that sold oxen and sheep and doves, and the changers of money sitting: And when he had made a scourge of small cords, he drove them all out of the temple ... and poured out the changers' money, and overthrew the tables ... and said ... Make not my Father's house an house of merchandise." (John II: 13-16)

Thus did the Roman New Testament put on the Jews the infamy of money changers and profiteering in the very heart of worship. This infamous slur on the Jewish people, who were the makers of religion, left its indelible scars on the reputation of God's own nation, and the Jews, after this Roman Christian Bible came to dominate all Europe, walked through their lives for two thousand years, not as God's chosen people, but as the foul remnant of a degenerated tribe.

The New Testament befouled the Jews as being money-mad, bereft of true faith. The New Testament marked the Jewish nation as treacherous Iscariots, greedy for silver—surnamed "Judas" to make sure everyone would identify the traitors as Judeans!

The stamp of greed and treachery was put on the innocent foreheads of all Jews by this vicious tale of God's son driving the money-changing Jews out of Solomon's Temple.

From this ugly invective in the New Testament stems the slanderous references to the Hebrews as usurers, double-dealers, defamers of sanctity, etc., etc. Nazism in all its ugliness was born in the anti-Semitic pages of the Roman Christian Bible, and found there a script for *Kristallnacht* and pogrom.

Muslims

are those who submit *(aslama)* to the will of God. Many thousands of "infidels" were put to flight or even death when they refused to submit. Yet Muslims have found room for Jews when Christians have had only the torture or gas room.

Only the Christian faith put to death by fire, sword or garrote even those tormented Jews who were ready to submit to Christianity, yet were burned alive or drowned with stone weights just because they were born of the same blood of Jesus.

It was the Moslems of Asia and Africa who helped

save some of Spain's Jews in 1492 from the fury of the Dominican and Franciscan torturers of the Inquisition.

Mythology

in Middle East and Mediterranean lands abounds with God-sired demigods. But only the Jesus legend weathered the tempests of time.

Will it, too, go with the wind?

New Testament

As has been said, Christianity is a doubtless lofty religion centering on the birth and life of a Messiah (Christ) of Davidian flesh and blood.

The fundamental bible of this Israel-born theology is called the New Testament, to differentiate it from the Old. The earliest versions of this evangelical text are in later-century Greek; the original, obviously Hebrew sources are unavailable, excepting one Aramaic sentence.

The persons of this great religious drama, as well as its miscellanea, correspondence, history, etc., as described or interpreted in all 39 chapters, are all, with one possible exception, Hebrews. Yet they are referred to only by their "Greek" names.

The New Testament is full of ancient Hebraic wisdom, but presented in Greek terminology which was certainly and totally alien to shepherds and fishermen like Shimon, Jochanan and so on. I doubt very much if Jeshu ben Joseph, the son of a Galilean carpenter, would have turned around at the call: "Jesus!" It would have been Greek to him, as to the others.

The New Testament abounds with expressions of Toraic simplicity on Love, Forgiveness, Kindness. Yet the Jewish infants of today will live out their years in the shadow of deadly persecution at the hands of the whole Christian world.

I refer not only to the German holocaust of the Hitler era. The rest of Christian Europe did little more than watch the kinfolk of Jesus being choked to death like infected cattle. The French Christians under Pétain, their beloved sage hero, the Hungarians under Horthy, the Slovaks under Father Tiso, the Austrians under Cardinal Innitzer, the Italians under Pope Pius XII, the Poles, the Ukrainians—they *all* helped fill the gas chambers of the German concentration camps.

The Christian world *in toto* was responsible for the massacre of a million Jewish children. Again, as in the era of the Spanish Inquisition, the Moslem protected Jewish life. At the end of World War II we find the Jews of Christian Europe obliterated, yet the Jews of North Africa and the Middle East remained untouched.

Christianity failed the Jew throughout its history. Why? Because Christianity despite its repeated admonitions of love and kindness toward all people, distinctly and in 102 places in its New Testament limits that love-appeal to Gentiles, marking "the Jew" as son of the Devil, as defiler of the Temple, as traitor, as money changer, as killer of God.

This lesson I just quoted from the Christian Bible has been beaten into the receptive minds of Christian children in church school and Sunday school. When a Christian child is confirmed, it is confirmed in unreasoning hate of "the Jew."

48

This explains why and how the Germans, perhaps the most cultured people of modern Europe, could gas a million Jewish children, starting with *German* Jewish children, while they never organized a similar program against the Christian children of the nations they were at war with, even such "traditional" enemies as France or Poland.

The New Testament has a noble message of love even unto the enemy for all gentiles; for the Jews it reserves in the words of the bishops of Rome who finalized its formulation in the fourth century, one outcry: Kill!

Ten million of the Jewish people were killed by the Christians during the last two millennia: Inquisitions, Crusades, pogroms, burning, hacking and drowning were the crude means of extermination used by the Church and its followers, their kings and nobles. Hitler's scientific advisors made it possible for Christian Europe to kill more Jews in ten years than the churches had in two thousand.

We are now at a temporary standstill of Jew killing. Yet I can hear the growl of the beast lurking nearby.

The New Testament has still not been cleansed of the vicious anti-Semitic propaganda inserted by the bishops of ancient Rome.

The New Testament still is inhabited by only two kinds of people, the Gentiles and the devilish Jews. Every Christian child is still exposed through evangelical Sunday school to the teaching that Jews are the "sons of the Devil and do their father's lust."

They are incubating today the same monsters of Jew-hate as they have done for the last two thousand years.

On every Christian altar rests this book that makes the Protocols of Zion and Hitler's *Mein Kampf* pale in ineffectiveness. The New Testament in its present form is far and away the most successful appeal to persecution and murder of Jews.

Until the New Testament is cleansed of its anti-Semitic references, pogrom against Jews must come again and again.

Christianity and Christianity alone has given birth to anti-Semitism. It is root and host of this ugly fungus. Cleanse the New Testament of its Jew-hate, and you will make an end to the killing of Jeshu's kinfolk.

Nuremberg Law

Adopted in 1935 with public acclaim throughout Christian Germany and within a few years accepted as religious (binding) in numerous other countries of Christian Europe (France, Poland, Austria, Hungary, Slovakia, etc.), depriving all Jews of all rights, including, ultimately, the right to live.

Protestant as well as Catholic clergy of Hitler's domain outdid themselves in abuse and derision of the Jewish people. Scholars in Catholic and Protestant universities lectured at length on the genetic depravity of the Hebrews, leaving no room for tolerance of God's people, while the silence of the Vatican left for the kin of Christ the abyss of the gas chamber as the natural, destined fate for the killers of God.

The basis for the Nuremberg Law, with all its bloody implications of public child murder, was established for two millennia by the Christian Bible (John VIII: 44): "And Jesus said unto [the Jews], you are [the offspring] of the Devil, and will do the lusts of your father [the Devil]. He [your ancestor] was a murderer from the beginning."

Joining hands across the centuries, the scribes of the New Testament and the Hitlerite lawmakers formed an unholy arch under which they led a million Jewish children and five million unarmed Jewish adults, men and women, to the gas chambers and torturous death.

Original Sin

If Adam ate an apple, what is that to you or me? And why do I need Jesus to take such "guilt" off my back?

Or is this a game of nonsense?

And from such a joke they spun a whole religion! God!!

Oxford University Wörterbuch

The repeated edition of the explanatory dictionaries of the Oxford University Press forcefully brought to my mind the German équivalent of Dictionary.

During the ten years of Hitlerism the German Christian publishers, as well as Austrian, French, Polish and Ukrainian sympathizers, would publish *Wörterbücher* to bring their readers up to date upon nomenclature and terminology.

The word "Jew" was one of the very few terms for which they were given space and a free poison pen to "define," "interpret," "evaluate," and finally determine the true meaning of the concept of a "Hebrew."

The Hitler lexicographers searched far and wide to find a welcome conglomerate of ugly synonyms for the

Jew: trickster, double-dealer, dishonest manipulator, etc., etc.

Only ten years ago I discovered in a number of British and French reference books that the German "scholars" were not the only ones who held an abattoir ideology of the Jews.

Linguistics and semantics dictionaries referred and still do define Jew as "dishonest trader," "unscrupulous cheat," "usurer," etc., etc.

I inquired from one of those academic publishing houses why they countenanced such slanderous pronouncements and was advised that they, the publishers, were only giving a clear picture of widespread usage of the term among the population of England and, especially, professional writers.

From the numerous examples the publishers supplied I had to admit that English journalists, teachers and writers were holding or upholding the opinion that Jews were dishonorable: Chaucer depicted them as blood-sucking killers of Christian children for ritual purposes; Marlowe, as poisoners of Christian wells; Chesterton, Belloc, and Eliot, as despoilers of Christian morality.

The eminent English philosopher, Francis Bacon, demanded that Jews wear a Jew-marker; Robert Burton refers to them only as the accursed ones; Thomas Browne as the contemptible offspring of Jacob; Shakespeare as usurers (in the manner of Jesus driving the Jewish money lenders out of the Temple); Daniel Defoe as crucifiers of the Lord; Alexander Pope as blood drinkers; even the Book of Common Prayer speaks of Jews with contempt. In short, British literature is befouled by Christian anti-Semitism.

For I could not help but admit that what those British writers expressed were merely variations on the malicious-Hebrew theme originally sounded in the New Testament:

Judas Iscariot sold God to Jewish priestdom and the Roman military; the Jews desecrated the Temple in Jerusalem by selling sheep, oxen, and birds, while other Jews, the money changers at the gates, cheated the populace. So the good Lord made a whip and chased the Jews out, leaving, I presume, the Chinese or Germans to mind the store!

My quarrel here is not with the British publishers who engage in such biased scholarship, but rather with the church-going masses of England, who support anti-Semitic bias and, following the example of the Christian Bible, divide the world into two kinds of people, the evil Jews and that decent lot, the rest of humanity.

Nothing in that vicious volume of England's best about the Lord Jesus calling himself a Jew; no mention that the minute minority of Jews have won almost half of all the Nobel Prizes; no hint that if not for Jewish doctors, half of the most virulent diseases would still decimate man. The Jew is a tricky money dealer, so declares England's dictionary. But the Lord says: They are My people. The dogs are barking, but the caravan of Israel walks on through the night of Christian hate.

Perfidious Jews

is the reference to the Hebrews in the holy, holy "Good Friday" prayer.

Pope John XXIII, the one and only Pope who did not accept the Satanic Jew hate of the New Testament, died in the process of cleansing the Christian Bible, Christian prayers and hymns of rapacious Jew hate.

Someday, maybe the Lord, the Father, will send us a Master Christian who will expel the words of hate and derision from the Christian canon and make the New Testament worthy of being bound in the same volume with the Torah.

Persecuting Jews

In the fifth chapter of John's Gospel, Christians must read: "The Jews persecuted Jesus and sought to slay him"—because Jesus was a healer on the Holy Sabbath.

What horrible people those Jews be, not at all like the gentle Romans, who on one day nailed seven thousand slaves to the cross!

Pilatus

The Roman procurator Pilatus is portrayed by the Roman New Testament of God's fleshborn son as a reasonable, fair-minded soul who pleads with the Jews to free the harmless pretender to the divine purple robe.

But the chief priests of Israel bellowed: "Crucify him, crucify him!"

This hyperbole of hate in the gospels has driven young churchgoers to tears of despair and deep suffering. Jesus, their gentle father image, is depicted as a fallen victim of Jewish bestiality, and the trauma of this horror deed against their "father" never leaves the young heart.

When Pilatus remonstrates to Jesus: "Am I a Jew? Thine own nation and the chief priests have delivered thee unto me," Pilatus is artfully given lines which at once absolve him, and shift blame to the entire Jewish people.

From this shrewd dramatic fabrication of conniving Roman bishops, springs the fear, hate and disdain for all Jews.

No explanations in later life or study can erase the wounding impact of this cunning dramaturgy to discredit the Jews and make them the central object of Christian greed for revenge.

Propaganda Fide

The various Bible societies distributed last year over two hundred million copies of the so-called Christian Bible, containing the same centuries-old anti-Semitic libels:

The Jews are sons of the Devil
The father of the Jews is a robber
The Jews are killers of God
The Jews are treacherous money changers
The Jews defile the Temple
When will this slander against God's people end?

Purgatory

Academically speaking, a Catholic and Anglican doctrine of temporal punishment of the recently departed for their sins of the flesh.

Since almost all sexual activity of the mature, old or even very young, is a venial sin in the warped judgment of Catholic clergy and sisterhoods, all of the departed—men and women and children—are "in" for a bit, quite a bit, of burning, roasting, toasting and sticking with pointed torches.

How even perverted theologians could think up so cruel and unusual a "judicial" process is beyond comprehension.

According to the theory and application of this Christian system of divine jurisprudence, every, but every, Christian except Holy Mother Mary has to go through the process of purgatory and come out ready for *paradisio,* perhaps with toes, breasts and genitals burned to a crisp, but now pure in heart and prepared to accept Jesus, carpenter and gentle preacher of the hills of Galilee.

I should think any thoughtful Christian would rather see his grandson or granddaughter die a Hindu or Buddhist or—God forbid!—a Jew, than be lightly roasted on a spit! But such is the imagination of emasculated clergymen and dehumanized nuns!

Sancta simplicitas!

They decorated their shrines and altarpieces with monstrous paintings of the hellish doings in purgatory—ugly little devils sinking their fangs into the breasts and buttocks of women and children, piercing eyes with glowing needles—a backdrop for generations of priests saying prayers and singing hymns, high clergy in full decor performing mass after mass, and preaching a sanguine flood of dramatic poetry, perpetuating the horror of Inferno from the time of Dante to the false priests of Nazi Germany.

Retribution

The Roman bishops interpret the fall of Jerusalem in the year 70 as God's punishment of the Jews for killing His son, Jesus, although the same Roman Legions also sacked Athens, Carthage, Alexandria, Syracuse, and so on, and so on.

With similar reasoning the Vatican refused to protest the butchery of millions of Jews in Hitler Europe, because it might, as Pope Pius XII philosophized, "trouble the conscience of the Christian German soldiers" and interfere with their soldierly obedience.

If Titus and Hitler are the right arms of the Lord, dealing out Divine justice, I would raise over the Catholic and Protestant Churches the Hooked Cross of the Nazis—as, indeed, was often done in the Hitler era.

Sacred Books

Koran, the holy book of the Moslems, deals in 114 chapters with man's submission to the will of God; Veda, the sacred scripture of the Hindus, offers blissful hymns in praise of God; Torah, guide of the Hebrews, tells the story of its people and their faith in the Lord; Teipitaka, Tathagata and other Buddha Texts all speak of the way to true virtue and the final enlightenment of Nirvana—all great religions are thus, all except Christianity.

The New Testament of the Christians is the story of a hanging, the crucifying and hanging of God at the behest of the Jewish people, belabored in such dramatic fashion that although the alleged event happened two thousand years ago, millions of Jewish children, women and unarmed men have been apprehended, poisoned, beheaded, burned alive until our day. The New Testament, the book of the love of Jesus, contains 102 vicious references to Jewish "perfidy and torture" and thus has become the greatest killer of all religions. Indeed, Christianity is the only religion that is so dedicated to the persecution of one nation, one people—the Jews.

While all major religions have adopted symbols of love, devotion or chastity, the Christian Churches have one basic symbol in their catacombs as well as on the pulpit: the cross-shaped gallows, often with a tortured, bloody body on it personifying the gentle Hebrew preacher as an executed criminal. This forever reminds all Christians that the Jew is their cardinal enemy and must be never-endingly punished and persecuted.

Jew-hate stems from the New Testament and its malevolent hatred of the Hebrew "God killers."

Such is the Christian theology of love!

Stolen Legacy

The Christian Bible consists 80 percent of the Old Testament from Adam to Sirach, and only 20 percent of Jesus-cult materials, from Jesus to Jesus' followers.

Most of the New Testament sayings, prayers and maxims are also taken from the old Hebrew wisdom literature renowned among people of the Middle East —except, of course, the miracles like walking on water, making wine out of water, bringing people to life who appear dead, feeding five thousand peasants and fishermen from a small basket, and so on.

Yet, the persons who put together in Greek the sundry gospels and letters known as the New Testament, it seems, did not feel it made enough of a Bible (book), so they attached it to the great, old, thick book known to all the Mediterranean nations as the Old Testament.

The early Christians claimed the Old Testament as *their* legacy, taken from the Jews by Jesus and given to them.

And the Jews, Jesus said, according to their new gospels, were and are, sons of the Devil, whom they serve.

So, not only were the Jews deprived of their legacy, they were simultaneously loaded with a new legacy as devils at large, to be punished forever for killing God.

Stone-Age Jews

Jesus said: I was here before Abraham; the Jews around him considered that statement ironical. "They took up stones therefore to cast at him." (John VIII: 59)

"Stubborn Jewry"

King David was a great warrior of the ancient Hebrew nation and a wise ruler of his people; his concern for neighbor countries was purely that of a defender of Israel's borders and security.

Why the Christian gospels make it a point that the coming Messiah (Christ) must be a descendant of this fiery royal swordsman is difficult to understand. If the message of Jesus the carpenter was for any and all listeners, why accept as a prerequisite of Messiahdom descent from a strongly nationalistic king?

Instead, the early Christians, wherever they propagandized, after failing to make inroads among the Jews, turned violently against them and accused them, the Jews and the Jews only, of being the archenemies of Jesus of Galilee. Even the crucifying Romans were treated in the Hellenistic manuscripts of the gospels as a rough but fair folk; the Jews were the actual killers of

God, making reluctant Romans carry out a most disagreeable task in executing Jesus.

The Christian gospel knows but two kinds of people—the Gentiles, and the ugly Jews, torturers of God.

In the long run, all Roman provinces and colonies, directed so by Emperor Constantine and his successors, accepted Hellenistic Christology—all but Israel. Israel rejected the principle of immaculate conception, fatherhood of a son by Jehova, vicarship of the heavens by Jesus the carpenter, sanctification of mother Miriam (Mary) and all the rest of the Hellenistic theology of the brand new religion fostered by the pagan ruler Constantine!

Israel said "No!" to Jesus, as it had said "No!" to Zeus!

There is not a single authentic manuscript, scroll, tablet or stone in Hebrew of the newborn Christian faith. The Jews of Palestine, Syria, and elsewhere totally rejected Jesusdom!

And the fury of the early pagan Christians turned on the Jews who had ridiculed a carpenter's son who was not really his son, and the miracles and magic of this professed son of God as mere Asian fakir tricks! The Jews were accustomed to magicians making wine out of water, walking on the waters of the sea, "healing the blind and lame," feeding a multitude with a hidden basket of fish, etc., etc.

The Hellenistic concept of their God, Jehova, siring a son with a woman betrothed to a Hebrew artisan was revolting to them, as was the "sinful" situation of Joseph, the "father in fact" finding his betrothed with child on the eve of their wedding.

What Greek pagans would accept with sophistication, the Jews would reject in totality. The presentation of Joseph the would-be father as a direct descendant of King David, to serve as another proof of the Messianic character of Joseph's son Jesus, all that merely enraged the Jews, who were in those early centuries furiously concentrating on the study of the Jewish Law in Jerusalem as well as Babylon and thus creating the immense archive of the Talmud. To the Jews who fought Roman dictators like Vespasian, Titus, and Hadrian to the very end, the Christian-sermon theme of God splitting Himself into Son and Ghost appeared as an offensive, implausible, and sinful throwback to the well-known and discredited Hellenistic Olympus.

The Hebrews abhorred the boundless polytheism of the Greeks with a god or godlet or demigod in every spring, cave or breeze.

The Romans, who took to Hellenistic romantic theology with ease and a bit of humor, simply renamed the Greek divinities in Latin and acknowledged a whole hierarchy of Romanized Olympians.

The Jews of the Mediterranean, forever rebelling against the immense militarism of the Caesars, would not give up their unswerving faith in God the One, the Eternal, the Invincible. Jews had lived for a thousand years before Jesus. Their Torah was accepted by the Roman authorities as *religio licita*.

The Diaspora after the fall of Jerusalem was just one of many in their turbulent history. This Semitic tribe lived in Iberia, in Sicily, in the south of France, at the environs of Rome, in North Africa. Yet, separated or together, Jews wanted no part of Jesus, the Son of God. The Jews were dead set against any anthropomorphization of Jehova.

On the other hand, the neo-Christian leaders needed something to back up their faith in young Jesus, so they packed wonder deeds and miracles around his sermons.

Searching further, they established or tried to establish an inner link between the ancient Old Testament and Jesus. Ah, now we have it—Jesus the descendant of King David, Jesus predicted by Hebrew prophets! So they concocted an instant *Kabbalah* (tradition) from Moses to Jesus. And thus they, as Christians still do today, were able to offer up 80 percent Old Testament and 20 percent New Testament as *their* Bible!

The Jews rejected and resented all of those new teachings and accused the early Christians of misusing the Old Testament by making it part of the Christian "Bible." But the new Christians needed the dignity and authenticity of the Old Testament to bolster their Neo-Hellenistic legends of God the Father and the rest of their anthropomorphic theology. The Christians even gave all legendary figures in their gospels Hebrew names, since no others in the Mediterranean world could surpass them in historic acceptance.

After appropriating the Old Testament of the Hebrews for the new Jesus religion, however, they declared all Jews God-killers for eternity, descendants of the Devil (John VIII: 44) doomed to perennial punishment, and themselves, the Jesus people, the only rightful inheritors of the Torah of Moses.

The ancient Hebrews remain holy men, the "precursors" of Christianity. Since the later Jews rejected Jesus, they are no longer "God's chosen people"; the Catholics are, and the Jews be damned and destroyed, man, woman and child!

Such was the verdict of the clergy in Christian Europe during the Nazi era. The hooked cross was visible next to the altar in all German and Austrian churches, Protestant as well as Catholic. Pope Pius XII personally approved the expulsion of the Jewish men, women and children to the gas chambers of central Europe. From France to Poland the spirit of early Christianity dominated—"Death to the Jews, killers of God." No Christian sword was raised to defend the children of Israel; only the crucifix went up, which shows the corpse of Jesus on the gallows.

Theologians

Theologians are those, one would suppose, who separate God from the fables. Yet the so-called "theologians" of early Christianity obscured God behind a farrago of second-hand fables, adding only one new, and sinister, character of their own.

The conquering Romans dismantled the outdated Olympic stageprops of their Greek slaves and replaced them with a new dramatic play, again with Godsired divinities, holy women, saints, sacrosanct vicars, miraculous happenings, witchcraft, magic and the awe-inspiring Hades.

The only difference between the old Roman play and the new was that Olympus had no devil, while Christian Rome fabricated a most handy, horny, clubfooted and taildragging monster-enemy of the new faith: the Jew.

Since the world loves to hate, it took to the newborn Christianity with passion and torch. No sooner was the Olympic Pantheon in Rome turned into a Christian cathedral, and the Holy Family painted on the walls and ceiling, than the bishop-inspired Christians took to burning Jews, synagogues, and scrolls.

The Church fathers gave the new Christians text and emblem to make the hate of Jews obligatory and worthy. Hate of the Jew became the living belief for each and every devout Christian, even as the tortured figure on the cross-shaped gallows became the universal symbol and reminder: Hate the Jew, he tortured our God to death.

The Olympic gods are long since a subject for operetta and farce, but the clever drama of the gospel is no joke. Ten million Jews were put to death by the faithful of the Roman bishops without a prayer, without burial.

The Roman fable-spinners are dead and gone, but their taint remains, unchallenged by their successors. Christian theologians invariably have retreated to their libraries when persecutions of Jews were initiated by the Church.

Where were the great professors and interpreters of Christian theology when Europe's Jewry was shoved into stoves on bread shovels? They were in academic seclusion, arguing moot points of religious semantics.

War

is like a sickness—you have to fight it if you want the innocent to remain healthy.

Warmakers like Titus or Trajan or Hadrian had to be resisted, as had Hitler or Mussolini or Stalin.

Those who avoid fighting the warmakers will reap not peace but servitude. Those who will not stoop to pick up the sword will bow before the whip.

Those who fled in distaste when Hitler's storm-troopers set out on the conquest of Europe were con-scienceless objectors.

They cared little about the world; they only wanted to escape personal discomfort and physical danger.

The great prophets in history were fighters, not escapists.

Word of God

No one has the ear of God except those who speak from the heart. And those who preach from their bile-ducts as if they shared the confidence of the Lord, are just confidence men of religion.

Zionism

Often in maturing years men yearn to return home, to their ancestral abode. In the Jewish people we find a nation that has awakened to such a profound and almost irresistible sentiment which now dominates their hopes and longing.

Those who ascribe to Zionists political greed for world domination do them a grave injustice. The Jews want to embrace their ancient lands, not use them as a springboard.

"Next year in Jerusalem"—this prayerful wish never really left the lips of God's most suffering people.

. . . *Summation*

When the Roman Emperor decided in the late 4th century to impose the Jesus cult upon all the inhabitants of the Roman Reich in all its provinces and possessions, he ordered the Roman bishops to prepare a Christian Bible with all the necessary prestige and stringent laws, rules and calendars.

Jesus, the Jewish preacher and carpenter, a man of gentle persuasion, was alleged to be a direct descendant of King David, as prophetic destiny required if, indeed, he was the true Messiah of the Jews.

There was nothing in the Mediterranean region that could match in status and dignity the universally known and respected ancient religion of Israel. So Rome simply took the Torah of the prestigious Hebrews, the people of the book, and made this most massive volume of Moses and the prophets into the basis of the new Christian Bible, directing the ecclesiastical scribes to add a booklet of the gospels of Jesus and a few epistles from his early followers. This supplement became the New Testament.

The most urgent requirement in the eyes of the Emperors who promoted the Jesus cult, was to unite the confused and polytheistic territories of the empire by establishing one homogeneous official religion.

Since the Mediterranean peoples knew of the

crucifixion of the gentle Hebrew rebel Jeshu ben Joseph by the Roman police forces in South Syria commanded by Pontius Pilatus, it was imperative for reasons of national discipline to free the Roman military of this stigma. Instead, the blame for the preacher's demise was laid upon the defiant Jews, who had refused openly and violently to knuckle under to the Roman dictate that would foist upon them a Hellenic series of divinities: God Jehovah, then a newly born son, then a mother of God immaculate yet married to a Jew, Joseph, and finally, a "Holy Ghost"—spiritual, yet with the face and body of a man.

The Jews from the very beginning of this church policy refused the trinity, deriding the whole idea of a God siring children with another man's wife. Egyptian, Mesopotamian, Hellenistic—polytheism had been known, and rejected, by the Hebrews since the days of Abraham and Jacob.

The Jews then as now believe in one God and Him alone and saw in the Christian theology nothing more than Hellenistic idolatry.

The Jews would not submit to Roman paganism. They fought it and, as at Massada in 136, they would rather die than serve false and alien idols.

For hundreds of years the Roman Christian Church has published and distributed millions of bibles, catechisms, and tracts in Latin, Greek and countless other languages—none in Hebrew—fixing the guilt for Jeshu's misery upon the shoulders of the Jews, and so even today from the center of the Christian Mother Church, the Roman Catholic hierarchy.

Jesus appears in the new Christian Bible as a man listened to by all the gentiles of the world—and persecuted only by the Jews.

The "Jesus" of the New Testament appears to recognize only two kinds of people, the gentiles and the monstrous Jews. And so we hear Jesus, son of the Jew Joseph, in the Roman New Testament speak thus to the Jews: You are offspring of your father, the Devil. He was a murderer from the beginning. He is a liar and the father of all deceit.

Do these lines not have the ring of Hitler or Torquemada?

The New Testament is the most vicious anti-Semitic play in history, surpassing *Mein Kampf* or the *Protocols of Zion*.

Of all the anti-Semitic writing the New Testament has been most effective, because it is reiterated as Holy Writ from cradle to grave. The Christian churches poison the minds of their young and old every Sunday—indeed, every day—with the "calumnies" of the Jews. The more devout a Christian, the more he or she gets the message. Every Christian child and adult is told of Jesus, the father image, and how the devilish Jews betrayed him, humiliated him, and finally had the Romans crucify him—indeed, when Jesus was already dying on the Cross, the slavering Jews demand that his bones be broken!

There is not an iota of truth to the story; it is not even a legend, but a devilish power play by the Imperial Roman church.

All anti-Semitism basically stems from the New Testament and cannot be eradicated until the Christian Bible is cleansed of the malevolent propaganda that darkens its pages.

M5